BRAMBLE

poems by

Brooke Herter James

Finishing Line Press
Georgetown, Kentucky

BRAMBLE

ACKNOWLEDGMENTS

Grateful acknowledgment to the editors of the following publications in
which these poems first appeared, at times in earlier versions:

Bloodroot Literary Magazine: "Sunnyside Up at the Sunrise Café"
Flapper Press: "Sheltering"
Orbis: "Found Poetry"
PoemTown 2021: "Ars Poetica"
Rattle: "While I Wait"
Tulip Tree Review: "The Obituary I Wish I'd Written"
Typishly: "Making Tracks"
Writing in A Woman's Voice: "And the Universe Resounds", "It's As If",
"Lunacy"

With gratitude to my many teachers: the Wednesday Poets, the Cigar
Factory Poets, Suzy Becker, Lynne Byler, Sharon Sorokin James, Waleska
James, Rennie McQuilkin and, finally, my beloved David, Sam, Megan, Peter,
Izzy, Frances, Ben, Hank, Linus, the donkeys and the dog.

Publisher: Leah Huete de Maines
Editor: Christen Kincaid
Cover Art: Meghan Bulmer / Alamy Stock Photo
Author Photo: David R. James
Cover Design: Elizabeth Maines McCleavy

Order online: www.finishinglinepress.com
also available on amazon.com

Author inquiries and mail orders:
Finishing Line Press
PO Box 1626
Georgetown, Kentucky 40324
USA

Table of Contents

FOR MY BROTHER AND SISTER

ONCE UPON A TIME

A table set out
in the beautiful garden
told us a story.

We knew time.

Time knew us as well,
among the bright flowerbeds
and the cool fountains.

IN BETWEEN

You had a rock
big enough to climb,
I had a secret path
down to the creek.

We mapped every
inch between
on bicycles,
in sneakers,

on Saturdays,
stopping only
at the Five-n-Dime
on Broadway

to spin allowances
into Turkish Taffy
and Sugar Babies.
Childhood lived

uninterrupted—
then Jeff liked you
and Robbie liked me
and I liked Jeff

and we didn't get up
as early anymore.
We hung around instead,
leaning against the slide

at the playground,
sitting on the swings
in our cutoff shorts,
watching being watched—

Noontide of in-between,
our shadows
zippered themselves up
underneath us.

THE OBITUARY I WISH I'D WRITTEN

My mother refused domestication. She sewed my Brownie badge on the right shoulder, which was the wrong shoulder. She put her cigarettes out in the mashed potatoes on her dinner plate and called for another Wild Turkey by wagging her finger up and down over the lip of her highball glass. She spent an entire week saying Supercalifragilisticexpialidocious instead of Fuck, and concluded that saying Fuck was much more satisfying. She once re-enacted Christina's World by lying prone in our backfield, arm stretched out in front of her. She stayed in that pose for two hours, waiting for my father to find her there. On my 11th birthday, she wrote EB White to request he send me a letter, it being his fault I was obsessed with pigs. He obliged. For her 50th birthday, she requested a boulder resembling a harbor seal be moved from a Maine beach to the stream in our suburban New York backyard. My father obliged. Then he left her for a French woman with skinny ankles. My mother lay on the couch for three days with a washcloth over her face and all the curtains drawn, after which she announced that he never *did* understand the difference between the *other side* and the *underside* of a leaf. She never remarried. Instead, she flirted with a man who drove a Subaru wagon with a volume of Shakespeare's sonnets on the backseat

and on her gravestone,
at her request: *I am my*
own woman, well at ease

DEAR ANNE

In the night, a sudden thunder of spring rain on the metal roof summons a train ride to Lake Geneva. We are just thirteen, best friends forever. Your parents press francs into our palms, enough for one plate of pomme frites at a waterfront café in Vevey. Later we hold hands, jump from the high board into the deep end of the pool at the school for hemophiliacs in Rolle, empty now for the summer. We race the halls, flirting with ghosts of pale, blood-letting boys. We wander through Les Diablerets' cobblestone streets aromatic with cows, cheese and chocolate. We climb out screenless windows onto the roof of our chalet, write postcards lying on our backs, waiting for supper.

Then there is the evening I mistake a green glass bowl of mothballs for peppermint candies—we lie awake listening as your parents whisper late into the night, certain it is my death they fear. But two summers later we return to bury your father. So much older we are, magic having drained from our veins, our pinky-swear promises now powerless, sunlight on the lake now suspect, the train to Vevey crowded and smelling stale.

Your mother sitting so upright, her black snap purse on her lap.

FLIGHT 684

The baby starts crying upon takeoff,
tiny gulps, then breathless intervals.
The eventual wailing accompanies
the steward's pantomime,
the captain's blessings for a safe flight,
the arrival of the beverage cart,
later the food trolley. The mother,
once allowed, leaves her seat
to journey with her infant
from row 39 to 8 to 39 to 8 to 39,
her eyes averted from the glares,
her ears trained only on the wailing,
not the weighted sighs, harmonious
murmurs of disapproval.
But soon she is crying, too.
Then a tall man in row 8 stands,
turns to face us, The Disgruntled, and says
STOP IT.   He says more, too—
about being a doctor and
inner ear pain—but all I hear is the
STOP IT   and I am in the backseat
of our station wagon driving to Maine,
pinching my best friend as hard as I can.
I am on the school bus, taunting
the boy with the lisp, the big ears.
I am shaking a report card in a child's face
saying *is this the best you could do?*
and to my mother on the phone
no wonder you're alone.
How many people have I made cry?

We pass through clouds,
over cornfields, swimming pools,
touch down on the shimmering tarmac,
collect our belongings,
exit the plane one by one.
At last the baby has fallen asleep,
but all I can think about
is how heavy my bag feels,
how uncomfortably still the air.

WE TRAVELED TO ROME IN FEBRUARY

The first whispers of Covid in Milan
notwithstanding. Pockets full of masks,
we promised our children we would stray
far from the swarm at the Sistine Chapel,
the too-close tables at the sidewalk cafes,
the legions lazing about the Forum—
promises easily forgotten for, oh,
the giddiness of stepping out
into thin sunlight with a whole day ahead
to happen upon Keat's tomb, Shelley's, too,
share a plate of carbonara midafternoon,
later a deep-fried artichoke and glass of beer,
perched on an ancient wall above the Tiber.
We knew trouble was in the air.
We saw the bold face headlines
on La Repubblica at every newsstand.
But like children playing tag in the dusk,
we wanted just one more frolic
before retreating inside
for the night that became a year.

SHELTERING
in the time of Covid19

Still life
here in Vermont
a solitary junco
half black
half white
sitting on the branch
half white
half black
against a backdrop of pond
black   rimmed with white
thank goodness for
the small red barn
in the lower right corner
of the scene

I imagine painting
over this canvas
apple blossoms
puffy clouds   a woman
in the foreground
faded yellow robe
leaning out her second
story window
to hang blue towels
and flowered sheets
on one end of a
never-vanishing cord
that travels from this hillside
to Milan   then Barcelona
Wuhan   Jerusalem   Sydney
Seattle New Orleans New York

An endless clothesline
adorned with the fabric
of the world billowing
outwards   music spilling
from all those unshuttered
windows   wafts of coffee
baked bread   squeals of children
running down hallways
pinging marbles on bare floors
dogs barking
I imagine painting
parakeets in wooden cages
singing while we wait

LUNACY

She woke at midnight
disoriented by the moon—
its light so bright as to
make shadows across the yard

like the certain brush strokes
of late afternoon sun
reaching past tree trunks
to lay patterns on the grass.

Is this madness?
to grope for shoes and robe,
to leave the house silently,
to stand on the front stoop

and wait—as if for a lover
to emerge from the silver gauze,
take her by the hand,
lure her out, like the tide?

Then a dog barks,
she retreats inside, lies
down in her empty bed,
listens to the clock tick.

But she refuses sleep—
not wishing to wake a second time,
only to know exactly where she is.

THE GHOSTS ARE OUT TONIGHT

All Hallow's Eve at the retirement home,
glass dishes of candy corn
on lace doilies all down the halls,
paper skeletons hanging
from the philodendron tree in the lobby,
the activities director slinks by *sassy tui*
my grandmother in black spider headband,
me with an orange marshmallow earring.
Down in the dining room
walkers pushed to the side,
tables strewn with orange and black confetti,
cauldrons of punch spilling vapor clouds
over plastic trays of ghoulish cookies.
We sit together near the band.
I tell her she is going to turn some heads tonight
but she can't hear—
she's already in the arms of her man
back for a spin across a moonlit square in Positano,
cigarettes still burning in ceramic ashtrays,
the Prosecco half drunk,
his hand on the small of her back
as they guise and soul the night away.

MAKING TRACKS

A neighbor stops by
to say his wife is leaving,
moving in with her sister,
just walked in the door one day
and said she wanted more from life.
It all came as a surprise, he tells us.
Still, I remember Christmas Eve
some years back when he gave her
that red Subaru wagon.
Long after their kids fell asleep
(I imagine he, too)
and the house went dark,
she was out doing donuts
in the fresh white snow.

ATONEMENT

I didn't think
about the masterpiece
I dismantled

yesterday afternoon
with the wide rim
of my straw hat

until this morning
when the sun angled
to reveal the splendid

re-creation—
and the spider who
must have been up all night

pulling a thread this way
then that until her web
was perfectly hers once again.

BEHOLD, THE DONKEY

Long after the ferris wheel stops whirling,
the kettlecorn stops popping,
the lop-eared blue ribbon bunnies
go home in the arms of small children
dressed in their 4H whites—
Long after the oxen stop pulling,
the merry go round ceases to spin,
the livestock fencing is taken down
and the last pick-up pulls out of the muddy field—
Long after all of that,
the donkey still refuses to budge.
What an ass, her owner mumbles
pulling hard on her lead
as three large men push from behind.
Come on you son of a bitch get in the damn trailer.
But the donkey refuses to budge.
And who can blame her?
A whole Sunday at the county fair
in the company of piglets and lambs,
admiring passers-by, children
reaching with their small hands
to stroke her ancient face,
or trace the outline of the cross
on her back. A taste of corn nuts,
peanut shells, an old hot dog bun.
And now, the first tiny star
appears in the deepening blue sky,
with the smell of hay underfoot,
headlamp lanterns, voices in the growing dark.
Get this, says one of the men, reading the sign
on her mostly dismantled pen.
*Thousands of years ago, it was she
who carried Mary to the stable,
heavy with child while Joseph walked alongside.*
The men stop pushing and pulling.
Maybe she just needs a moment, for God's sake,
says one to the others. *It was quite a day, after all.*

A SUDDEN GUST

Today a sudden gust
lifts the clothes on the line sideways—
your tell-tale socks rise leeward,
my pale blue sundress luffs,
your striped pajama arms
encircle the waist of my lace nightie,
holding on for dear life
as azure beach towels
tack to starboard, then to port
and bright white sheets fill with
a riotous snapping and flapping of cotton.
The whole ensemble tests the rigging.
Lines grow taut against the mast,
now heeling, heeling, heeling—
then sudden calm.
All that was listing is righted,
all that was once aflutter
drifts down into repose,
ready to be folded and put away.

SUNNYSIDE UP AT THE SUNRISE CAFE

Oh, to be the fried egg
on the blue plate
sliding down the counter
with my sunny side up,
me and my homefry friends,
maybe my buddy toast
all buttered on one side,
Marilyn and Elvis winking down
from over the pass-through
as I come to a perfect stop
in front of you.
You've got the daily news
opened on your right,
knife and fork on your left &
you say, *Hey, Dolores, how about some Joe?*
& she fills you right up to the brim.

I know it's not much,
but it's not nothing either,
to be part of that story,
to be there at the start
of each day—when you say
You're a good egg, Dolores,
I should have married you
when I had the chance,
and she laughs
her beautiful laugh.

ARS POETICA

He lifts long strips
of wood, bends them
slightly at each end,
tucks their edges,
clamps and glues,
nails and sands,
varnishes and paints
as the moon climbs
past the bay of the barn.
The donkeys linger,
the chickens cluck
and I, on a stool
in the corner—
sit mesmerized–
as he coaxes
a seventeen-foot wherry
from a heap of boards.
He, who says
he can't write a poem.

WHILE I WAIT

At the sidewalk café
a white-haired man
asks for coffee, hot,
cream, no sugar.

His daughter touches his sleeve
and points—the cranberry scones
in the glass case—
your favorite, remember?

His granddaughter splashes
in the ceramic dog bowl
brimming with cool water
on the porch step

where I sit shielding my eyes
from the sun with a menu,
the salmon pink impatiens
in the clay pots tremble

when a concrete mixer rumbles by,
spinning its vanilla and orange striped drum.
Look, I whisper to the little girl,
a swirled ice cream cone on wheels.

Late August drifts by,
settles on my sun-warmed knees.
A friend of mine died
last week, I say to no one

as I wait for you to cross the street,
waving as you come.

FOUND POETRY

Had I not crossed
the room at just
that moment,

had I not glanced
out the front window
and slightly to the left,

I would not have seen
the poem
in the crabapple tree—

its branches flush
with robins, barn red
against unexpected spring snow,

then gone, swelling the sky
with meter and rhyme
all their own.

COULD IT BE THAT OVERNIGHT

the peas have ventured across the garden path
to mingle with the beans—
(wasn't it just yesterday they were planted?)
& the zucchini vines have dared to embrace
the tomatoes & the oregano has grown
so voluptuous with blossoms as to draw
the attentions of honey bees and paper wasps?
Corn stalks, once so gangly, are tossing
long brown tassels behind their ears,
their stalks suddenly tall enough
to gaze over the fence at the field beyond?
So this is how it happens, I think—
in that moment we look away,
our children grow.

THE DOG SHARES HIS LIFE WITH ME

Just as surely as he hears
my covers pulled back,
I hear him leap from his bed,
gallop down the stairs,
careen across the mud room floor,
skitter over pine boards,
arrive at my side
just seconds before
my bare feet feel for the rug.
Good Morning, his body sings out,
corkscrewing tail, wet nose in my hand.
I have so much to tell you
about the orange crescent moon
over the mountain last night,
the lonely owl in the pine woods,
the coyotes beyond the barn,
the donkeys leaving their stall
in darkness to amble through
the long damp grass in early light.
Hurry, his body sings out.
I have so much to show you—
the bunny in the raspberry patch,
the wood ducks on the pond,
the tennis ball under the porch,
the hole I will dig in your flower bed,
how high I can jump for the
sparrows in the crabapple tree,
how fast I can chase butterflies
over the lawn.
Let's go, his body sings out.
You and me
now, quickly,
please.

HEART LIKE A HOME

This room is awash
in skates, scarves,
hats, hockey pucks,
dog bowls, jackets
fallen from hooks,
grocery bags crammed
into corners, chewed
tennis balls, bits of hay
stuck to sneakers,
legos under the rug,
beanie babies in backpacks,
and, through it all,
the distinct perfume
of, somewhere,
a rotten orange—
you worry if you can
love the baby
on the way as much
as the child already here—
and I say just look at this room
bursting at the seams
but never too full
for another pair of mittens.

AND THE UNIVERSE RESOUNDS

Look what I can do!

proclaims the light outside
the kitchen window
where I stand still
in pajamas waiting
for the coffee to brew.
The hillside is ablaze,
Rothko orange beneath
a sky so deep slate blue,
I want to wake my husband.
Then the phone buzzes,
and a photo appears
of my six-week old grandson
in a turquoise-striped onesie,
smiling full on
for the first time.

Look what I can do!

THINGS LEFT TO BE FOUND

I stoop to pick up a wooden block
and see a smudge of dog nose
next to your tiny hand print

on the sliding glass door,
left there one year ago,
perhaps on a rainy afternoon.

You might have been staring out
at waves breaking or your plastic pail
tipped by the wind or waiting

for the grilled cheese,
dipped in ketchup,
you will share with the dog.

I contemplate spotlessness
but, oh, tiny handprint
on the glass wall of my summer cave—

vision quest of a one-year-old
on a rainy afternoon—
may you last forever.

GIVING WAY

She stands still
at the garden's edge
watching me pull
withered beans,
frostbitten zinnias,
the last of the carrots,
an occasional potato.
I pile dried leaves
over barren beds,
put my trowel
in the red bucket and sit.
I don't dread this day. Besides,
it was a good summer,
I say, and she, my sunflower,
nods her head,
shedding the last of her seeds.

TWIG MATES, YOU AND I

We unfurl soft sails
in early spring, shiver

through cool breezes, still wet
from soaking rain, then bask

between blankets of summer's heat.
We welcome the visits of passing

warblers, the incessant gossip
of crickets and love-starved tree frogs.

We flash our undersides,
compare lobes and veins,

whisper of the deep greens
draining away all around us

until we, too, recognize fall
in the school bus passing

beneath our bough. We watch
a rogue leaf fly by, charting her course

over the white pines. We hold
even tighter as our edges

start to harden around our
newly brittle selves. An October day

brings a northwest gale and you let go—
I follow. We swirl, twirl,

pirouette around one another
until you sail on a westward current

over the barn, beyond the pond
to the pasture below and

I journey east through the orchard,
across the dirt road, drift down

between granite boulders,
at last at rest in the bardo

with so many long days ahead
to wonder will you meet me on the other side.

LATE WINTER WINDOW SHOPPING IN VERMONT

The UPS truck grumbles down our rutted drive,
a rare sighting this time of year—
Christmas past, no birthdays until July.
The packages are all addressed to me.

Scarlet red gabardine cape with matching boots and hat?
my husband's eyebrows inquire.

An impulse buy, I explain, brought on by the cardinal
in the bare branches, his fire-engine flash like a dare
against winter's endless white and frigid embrace.

A faux-fur tawny boa and black leather gloves?

Suggested by the lusciously fuzzy squirrel
hanging on the suet. Such delicate paws! I offer.

A necklace of felted beads, taupe, slate and vanilla?

You know how I do love juncos.

We walk the muddy road together after supper,
his hand in mine. And when we get back home,
we agree: It's time to take the birdfeeders down.

HINDSIGHT, 2020
—Year of the Pandemic

I had twelve whole months to learn Italian,
perfect a sourdough starter,
go back to practicing piano,
write long letters with a pen dipped in ink,
read Tess of the D'Urbervilles and Moby Dick,
make photo albums for each of the kids,
knit you an Irish sweater with a cap to match,
clean out the junk drawer
and the closet under the stairs.
Alas, don't ask how I spent my days
and I won't ask how you spent yours.
Still, remember this—
We had dinner together every night
at our little kitchen table. We survived.

ONE MORNING THE ROAD LETS GO

Ice into mud,
we step outside, wave
to the mailman as he sets
his first deep tracks.
What was grey is now honey—

worth saving, hoarding—
the light that pours through,
forces open screen doors,
beckons us to the front stoop
as the dog uncurls.

The donkeys stand far from the trees,
the metal roof groans its pleasure
and flies crawl from chinks.
We drink the light in gulps, greedy
for the lengthening afternoons.

IT'S AS IF

Under the full worm moon of March
the meadow mice scamper
across a field of light,
the ewe leans her wooly chin
on the split-rail fence,
the pig ambles out of doors
on her cloven hooves,
the donkey refuses
to lie down in the hay
and I, in my bare feet,
stand in the doorway
of soft midnight,
in a moment that opens
wide like a prayer
under the first full moon of March—
it's as if we can hear the sap rise.

Brooke **Herter James** won her first creative writing award in eighth grade and her second many decades later. In between, she followed a circuitous path that included college, graduate school, public health nursing, and raising a family. Ten years ago, she remembered that grade school story and decided to circle back to what she likes to do most. *Bramble* is her fourth collection of poems. She is also the author of the children's picture book *Why Did the Farmer Cross the Road?* She is a devoted member of both the Wednesday Poets (a group of writers from New Hampshire and Vermont) and the Cigar Factory Poets (a collection of writers from all over!). She lives in a very old house in Vermont with her husband, two donkeys, four chickens and one dog.

Lightning Source UK Ltd.
Milton Keynes UK
UKHW012008111022
410338UK00003B/20